Enwrapped in Grace

A Journal of God's Grace

Enwrapped in Grace

A Journal of God's Grace

ENIBOKUN TAYO

For all the women out there, who are struggling either with raising a child or living out a difficult marriage, your rest is coming...

CONTENTS

AN UNEXPECTED TREASURE

Before I formed you in the womb I knew you... (Jeremiah 1:5)

O n a bright sunny market day morning in June 1962, Blessing was born to a young girl in her early twenties, unmarried, in a small village called Opoji, deep in rural South South Nigeria. It was a community where girls who got pregnant without being married were ostracized.

Blessing's mother, Dorcas, who had become pregnant while still at school – was not an exception. She was thrown out of the family home by her mother, who felt terribly ashamed. Rejection was everywhere, so with nowhere else to go, she found refuge in the house of an elderly woman who served as the community midwife and took in young girls who were in trouble.

This was a season of darkness for Dorcas, but just as the word of God says treasures in darkness... Blessing indeed was that hidden treasure for Dorcas in her darkness.

As Blessing was born, things began to change. Blessing was the first grandchild to her paternal and maternal grandparents, and her paternal grandfather was so very excited about her birth that he wanted to welcome her into the world properly with the fruits of his harvest. He was a rich farmer. Thereby making Blessing and all other children with the midwife live in plenty. Such a blessing he was!

They were not estranged from their family for long. Dorcas was greatly missed by her three younger brothers who, while they were with the midwife, brought her gifts. Eventually, Blessing's grandmother also regretted her actions – apologized and brought her daughter and granddaughter back home.

In fact, for the first few years of Blessing's life, it was her grandmother taking care of her and that included when Dorcas left home to Benin City for greener pastures. Dorcas earned money doing odd jobs for people. Then, good fortune came her way when she met a wealthy woman, Miriam, who owned a Filling station. She immediately took a shine to Dorcas and gave her a job as a live-in housekeeper and nanny. Her children came to love Dorcas so dearly.

Miriam took Dorcas under her wing, instructed that Blessing be brought to Benin City, and the rest is history. She indeed was a destiny helper raised by God, assisted Dorcas to start her own small business and rented her own one room, where she lived with Blessing and her three brothers whom she had brought down from the village so they could learn a trade and find work. That is to say, five of them lived in one room.

Dorcas herself began selling printed fabric – she carried several pieces on her head and walked around the city to find buyers. Then, she graduated to selling from a small shop, and she became a contractor supplying building materials to different companies.

Dorcas was desperate for Blessing to have all the opportunities she never had as a child and dedicated her life to providing for Blessing and taking good care of her. Dorcas overprotected her child both from society and other children, not wanting her to be subject to any bad influences. So, she would be sure to be back home from selling at her shop to greet Blessing when she returned from school.

They would eat together and then as she started her homework, her mother would lock her in and go back to her shop. There was surely a longing to be like the other children. But as she grew older, the reason behind those actions became clearer: her mother just wanted the best for her.

Blessing continued to spend her holidays at her grandmother's despite being in Benin City. It was with her grandmother that she first learned about the Christian faith. Her grandmother served idols, but when missionaries came to Opoji, her village, she started helping them – cleaning their houses, sweeping the church, doing their washing – and in the process, she met Jesus Christ. She always took Blessing along to do all of these and by the time she was four, she could say the Lord's Prayer by heart in her native dialect.

Blessing's grandmother did so much to impart the values of hard work, caring for others, and loving people just as they are, that when she died, Blessing was indeed devastated. She had just turned 14.

A memory often came back to her... It was of the missionaries and her grandmother gathering up all her idols and carrying them to the bush to be burnt. Also, her mother Dorcas saying that in the midst of that mourning, she slept one night and was saying out loud, "Lord, I will serve you, I will serve you until the very end," over and over again.

Dorcas did not know the Lord, so when she was seeking protection for herself and her daughter, she went everywhere she thought possible to find it, even to the Juju priests who, of course, saw it as a way to make money out of her. And they sure did that greatly. She also visited several gynaecologists for treatment, resulting in the birth of a son who died when he was a few years old. Thus leaving Dorcas with no other option than to give Blessing the best start in life as she could.

SCHOOL YEARS

Train up a child in the way he should go.... (Proverbs 22:6)

Blessing had her first experience of schooling when she was four years old. She was one of about twenty children who were gathered each day by a local woman, given black slates and chalk, and seated under a tree to learn basic arithmetic and letters. Private boarding schools were seen as the best places to educate children in Nigeria in the 1960s. Dorcas worked extra hard to put her daughter in one of those schools. So, at six years old, Blessing was sent to a private boarding school in Benin City.

Dorcas continued to work hard to provide for Blessing and take good care of her. Dorcas registered with a family doctor, whom she took her daughter to whenever she fell ill. Despite not knowing either of them well, the doctor offered to start paying the 16 shillings a year for Blessing till she completed her primary education. He was a destiny helper sent by God.

The school was owned by a woman who was married to an Anglican Priest. Her family lived downstairs and all the children were upstairs; each night, she would pray over them and prophesy on them and on Blessing specifically. She can boldly say her prayers had an impact on her life in some way.

When Blessing went to secondary school, which was another boarding school, she was in for a shock. Tasks like fetching water, cleaning and ironing her clothes, which she was used to her mother taking care of, were now her responsibility. As well as having to fetch water for herself, she also did for the senior student she shared a bunk bed with. The school was very strong on discipline. As little as not ironing her uniform properly, for example, would lead to some form of punishment.

Blessing was not from as wealthy a family as some of the other students. However, because she was an only child, she had more provisions from home than the others most of the time. Her mother Dorcas was worried she was too thin, since she did not like many of the meals served at school (particularly the beans, as it was not uncommon to find insects in it).

Hoping to encourage her daughter to eat more, Dorcas would send plenty of food. Miraculously, Blessing learnt to share which, being an only child, she was not used to. She always worried that her provisions would run out and the other children would break into her cupboard every now and then Distraught, she was! But nothing could change that.

At first, Blessing chose to live with the housemistress to avoid being bullied. However, her mother saw that as being pampered and encouraged her to move back into her dormitory so as to have the experience. She was certainly right; being in the dormitory with others shaped her life and character. The discipline there taught her to be focused, to stay out of trouble and follow the rules. She learned when to speak and when to keep her thoughts to herself.

Her mother would come almost every weekend to see her and bring whatever she needed. When others in her dormitory were sick, she would look after them, fetch their water and do their duties for them.

Everyone saw her as different, just as her mother always said. So Blessing began to play with the idea of becoming a Nurse, but the problem was, she could not stand the sight of blood!

However, school held a sadness for Blessing, one that was amplified on Visiting Day, which was the day both parents visited their children. Most fathers were there on that day, and that depressed Blessing a lot since she did not have a relationship with hers. It was quite an issue that affected her seemingly beautiful life, and the other children would call her a "bastard" at any given opportunity.

Their taunting left her feeling timid – reluctant to speak in class most times. She knew she lacked nothing materially; even so, life was empty without her father. A void no one could fill. Thus, at that young age, Blessing promised herself that when she had children, she would remain married to their father, no matter what.

Though she was admitted to study Nursing, she opted for Education and became a teacher because of her love for children and a strong desire to impact their lives.

At the College of Education, Blessing studied French, which gave her the opportunity to do a session at the University of Abidjan, in Ivory Coast. It was the first time she ever left the shores of Nigeria. The journey itself did not go smoothly as the bus carrying them to Abidjan in Ivory ran out of fuel in Ghana. To complete the journey, the Nigerian ambassador came to the rescue.

After having her three children, she went on to University to do a B.Ed in French... And finally a Masters in Special Needs Education at a London University to be able to support the children in that group, particularly in her retirement years.

FINDING LOVE AND FACING LOSS

Known unto God are all his works... (Acts 15:18)

I t was not long after she came back that she met Hamza, the man who would become her husband. They met in Warri while he was doing his National Youth Service and Blessing was in her final year at the College of Education. Hamza had returned from France, where he studied Metallurgy, and they met through a mutual friend who was also doing her National Youth Service.

They continued to be just friends until about two years later when Blessing had done her own National Youth Service and was back in Warri.

They soon ran into problems: Blessing's mother did not approve because the region Hamza was from was associated with pagan practices and witchcraft. Hamza's mother did not approve either because Blessing was from another part of the country, and she did not speak the same dialect as Hamza.

His mother, Asake, insisted she didn't understand English, which was a great lie as Blessing would later find out from Mobo, Hamza's half-brother.

Anyhow, the two mothers could not stop the couple from spending time with each other, and after a couple of years, they gave in and said it was better for them to get married than to be living together when not married.

The two were married on 26th April 1986 in Benin City, when Blessing was 25 and five months pregnant with their twins. But what should have been a happy occasion for her was marred by the apparent dislike of her in-laws: Hamza's whole family arrived after the wedding, with the exception of his immediate younger sister, who ran in just at the time for the signing of the marriage register. A moment of sadness for Blessing and anger for Hamza.

Hamza's mother ignored Blessing for the whole day, while the words of one of his sisters that day – shouted across to her – continued to echo in her mind forever more: "Blessing na our house you go sleep today o."

At that time, Hamza was working for the Nigerian National Petroleum Company and a couple of months after the wedding, the company sent him to Italy for a training course. They did not think there was anything to worry about as the pregnancy had gone on without any problems. Hamza was still away in August when she went into labour while with her mother-in-law, and life took a tragic turn.

The labour took hours and in a heartbreaking turn of events, when the first baby was delivered, she was stillborn. She was then hurried into theatre, the doctor desperately trying to save the surviving twin with an emergency cesarean. Despite their efforts, when the second child was brought out, she gasped and gave up, compounding the devastating losses in a time that should have been filled with joy.

From then on, it was Blessing who was fighting for her life. She had a generous episiotomy and a very rough laceration from the cesarean, leading to severe blood loss. It was past midnight and all the blood banks were closed. So, her doctor began the search for blood that night, waking up different people to no avail.

Dr Pricentia, a Surgeon who owned another hospital, gave the one pint of blood he had in his blood bank. Thus saving Blessing's life and keeping her going until the blood banks opened the next morning for them to get the extra three pints she needed.

For the next fortnight, she stayed in hospital, too weak to get out of bed and overcome by the feeling that everything was pointless. When she was physically well enough to go home, her mother and mother-in-law stayed with her while she waited for Hamza to come back from Italy. Emotionally, she was broken – each day, she would cry and cry about her babies; all the while, far away, Hamza had no idea what had happened.

At that time, there were no mobile phones; contacting him was just impossible. So when he returned from Italy a month later, he was expecting to meet their babies. However, that was not to be. Hamza came excitedly into the house, only to be told what had happened. All around him were bags full of things for the babies which he had brought from abroad, and yet to arrive were all the bulky baby items which he had shipped. These items turned out to be painful reminders of their loss that they had to lock them away.

In his grief, Hamza turned cold towards his wife – each day, he got up, went to work, came home, ate, and went back to bed, with barely a word said to her. He started drinking heavily and sometimes would not come home until the early hours of the morning. Over time, the couple grew closer again, but cracks had begun to show in their relationship which would become clearer years later.

COMING TO CHRIST

If ye abide in me and my words abide in you... (John 15:7)

Blessing's faith journey remains her greatest gift in life, for which she remains eternally grateful to her grandmother and the baptist Deacon who led her to Christ. So her life has been a battle of thrones against the throne of God in her life, and she can confidently say that God has continually caused her to triumph as His word says in 2 Corinthians 2:14. So will she say it was worth it? Yes, and confidently so.

So, while Blessing was still pregnant with her twins, a Deacon from the Baptist church kept coming to her to tell her to give her life to Christ. "The Lord wants to use you, stop running," he'd say. And Blessing kept replying, "Stop harassing me or I'll tell my husband." Their paths had last crossed a fortnight before Blessing went into labour. They were at a petrol station and he said to her, "Please, I'm begging you. Do not let something bad happen to you before you come to Jesus."

Blessing did not care, but she took his business card, which he offered her in case she changed her mind. Then, a couple of days before the delivery, a neighbour who lived directly opposite also told Blessing she had an evil foreboding. It was only after the loss of her twins and her own near-death experience that she knew they both spoke the truth.

Be that as it may, Blessing still felt bitter towards God for the death of her babies: "Why didn't He save even one?" she kept saying. When her fellow teachers told her that her pain would go away if she gave her heart to Jesus, and that soon she would have more children, they just made things worse.

"What possible logic is that?" Blessing thought. Months went by, and on 27th April 1987, Blessing was alone and she said, "Lord, I am tired. I lost my babies. I really would love to get pregnant again. But I don't want to go through the same thing again." As she was talking, all of a sudden, it felt like a cloud filled the room. She felt something welling up inside her, and laughter just poured out of her... endless laughter. Then it felt as if she was falling asleep, and she heard a voice say, "My hand is upon your life. You will serve me. So, stop running." A glorious encounter.

She was still on the bedroom floor when her husband returned home; she pretended that she had just fallen asleep. Afterwards, all Blessing could think about was going to church come Sunday. Hamza did not want to go with her, so he dropped her off at the Baptist Church, where she knew

Deacon was the organist. He saw her walking into the church and started playing the song: "He has promised, He will never fail; I will lean on him..."

The Deacon, whom Blessing had previously dismissed, became like a father to her. He helped her understand the Bible through the Bible Study group at his house, and he taught her to pray everywhere all the time, and about everything. Years later, she is able to look back on the Deacon's advice and see how so many prayers she had prayed had been answered by God. From then on, she found hope and a new lease of life and began to experience God's power and see His glory.

MOTHERHOOD

For this child I prayed... (1 Samuel 1:27-28)

Next to Blessing's salvation was the gift of her three lovely sons through whom she has learnt life and living even better. God's grace upon their lives is beyond her comprehension. In them, God has continued to do all things well, as in Mark 7:37.

As soon as Blessing gave her life to Christ, she prayed earnestly to have children. Did God do it? Yes, he did – to the letter. She prayed that the Lord would give her her twin girls back as single babies and as boys. That when the oldest boy was celebrating his first birthday, the second baby would be one month old. Did He do it? Oh, He did it, making a name for Himself.

Blessing had her first son, Azariah, in May 1988 and her second son, Paul, in April 1989. Then she prayed, "Lord, this is a handful! Let my third child come when the second one is three years old." And so it was – Barnabas was born in February 1993. Through each child, God gave a different gift

– with her eldest son, God taught her the meaning of unconditional love; with her second son, God taught her patience; and with her baby, God gave her joy unspeakable.

Blessing wanted five children being an only child, but the odds were against her because her experiences in pregnancy had been full of spiritual battles, showing forth in dreams. In addition to this, on the conception of her last son Hamza had told Blessing that he never told her he wanted another child with her, so stopping after having three was the best option.

These experiences drew her closer to God whenever she was expecting: the fear of impending danger meant she constantly prayed. God showed Blessing many things about her children in dreams and visions, all these strengthened her faith. When she held her first son soon after he was born, Blessing saw a picture of him with a stethoscope around his neck, so she prayed over him, and he indeed became a medical doctor. The second, she held him and saw him in an overall... an engineer was made by God. And the third had a wig, whom God made a lawyer.

Another instance was of her first son rolling a suitcase across the ocean, so she prayed that they would be able to study abroad and all three eventually did, in the UK and the USA.

After Azariah was born, Hamza refused to let their eldest son be dedicated in church, deeming it too showy. His decision caused Blessing real heartache because she wanted to give thanks to God for Azariah's birth, considering the loss of their twin girls born before. Fortunately, Hamza had gone ahead to arrange Paul's dedication with Blessing's Pastor as soon as she gave birth. when it came to their youngest, She just took charge and went on with the dedication.

She continued praying for her husband's salvation, but she prayed much more about their financial situation: Hamza had grown up in extreme poverty and Blessing wanted to make sure their children had a better life so looking back years later, she regretted not praying more for his salvation than for wealth.

Blessing also became mindful of a pattern in her mother's family where couples normally broke up after the first child – the women would often go on to make a success of themselves, but they never had another child and were never able to remarry. She begged God to break that pattern as she was determined to stay with her husband out of obedience to God and so that her children would have a stable, well-rounded life.

At her mother's insistence, despite not wanting to go back, Blessing went back to School after having all her children to do a Bachelor of Education degree. Her mother looked after her children just as she had promised. She paid her daughter's fees and provided all she needed, which Blessing remains ever so grateful for.

When she finished and it came to binding her project, she didn't want to ask her mother for anything else since it was a small amount. However, when she asked Hamza for it, he said he didn't have it. A friend of Hamza, who would normally visit with his fiancee on Sundays then, whom he married, was there, and pleaded with him on Blessing's behalf, but he still refused.

Not long after, on another Sunday, Hamza decided to embarrass his wife with the same couple who were Catholic. While they were all talking after church, Hamza turned to his friend and said, "You know, my wife doesn't like your Catholic Church." The friend didn't utter a word; Blessing's husband had succeeded in humiliating her. A marriage gone sour. Her heart began to grow cold.

LIFE ON BONNY ISLAND

He Himself has said, "I will never leave you nor forsake you."
(Hebrews 13:5-6)

B
lessing's prayer for financial security was answered
when in 1998, after 12 years of living in Warri, they
moved to Bonny Island. While Hamza was working
for the Nigerian National Petroleum Company, his highest pay
was still not admirable. But when he was seconded to Nigeria
Liquified Natural Gas (NLNG) to work as a project engineer
on the NLNG project, his salary suddenly meant a life of
luxury. The kind the family had not seen.

Blessing's faith took a quantum leap after an initial struggle of
not having a place of worship. Eventually, that settled.

Hamza's contract initially was for 19 months, so it was
decided he would move to the Island while Blessing and the
children stayed in Warri. That September of 1998, her two
older sons were sent off to boarding school in Port Harcourt,
and her youngest, Barnabas, was just starting primary school
so they were home together. The other women whose

husbands worked for the same project told her that Hamza's contract would certainly be renewed and that she should move to Bonny Island to be with her husband – otherwise, her house would become a brothel.

Blessing took time to pray and felt led by God to move to Bonny Island, not wanting to make the decision based solely on her own feelings. She was convinced she needed to follow her husband. So, in December 1998, Blessing moved from Warri with Barnabas to Bonny Island, only to be met with Hamza's fury. Blessing had thought it would be a pleasant surprise for him to come home to find his wife and son, but she was dismayed to find that he was outraged.

Blessing soon learned from the other women in the neighbourhood that men had been meeting their girlfriends and mistresses at Hamza's house.

For the next eight months, from December 1998 to August 1999, her husband hardly spoke to her. He'd leave for work and come home just to eat dinner; that was their only interaction. Determined to create a good life for her family, put all her focus into home-schooling her youngest son.

One of Hamza's friends was setting up a home-school group – the idea was for half a dozen families to club together to pay a teacher's salary and for them to be taught in the neighbour's house. Then, when NLNG had finished building a school on the site, these children would be all ready to enrol.

The only necessary requirement was for the child's father to fill and sign a form and then pay 3,000 Naira needed for the Teacher. But Hamza refused and said they should go back to Warri where he left them. Her neighbours kept asking why her son was not attending the class, but she was too ashamed.

Blessing looked to God again for a way forward. Every month, her husband would spend five days in Lagos – the NLNG employees were given this time off because for the rest of the month, they were working from 6 a.m. to 6 p.m. – and so she prayed and fasted while he was away. "God, if you are the God that I serve and if it was your will for me to come here," she prayed, "when my husband comes back, he will sign this form and he will give us the money for the school." She felt God's assurance that the matter was settled.

When Hamza returned, Blessing cooked him his dinner, put the admission form by his plate with a pen and asked him again to sign it. She said she could pay the money herself but that she wanted it to come from him because that was his place.

"It is OK to ignore me," she said, "But we cannot let our son suffer for whatever anger you have against me; let the child reap the benefits of the job." Hamza did not reply. He stood up silently, washed his hands, took the pen and signed the form, and then brought out 3000 Naira. Again, God answered her prayers.

Still, he found ways to undermine her. When NLNG were able to set up a school, they were looking to hire teachers. She did not think of applying – she assumed they wouldn't hire her since her husband already worked for the company. Then, when his friend who was running the school came to their house and suggested Blessing should apply, Hamza asked, "Is she qualified?" He seemed to forget that she had a degree in education and had taught in secondary schools for ten years before retiring voluntarily.

At the time, Blessing was making money from buying and selling goods from abroad – she would go to the UK to buy clothes, to Italy to buy shoes and bags, or to Dubai to buy gold and then sell back in Nigeria. Her business was booming. But Hamza always wanted to put her down and he would say, "Body is catching you because you are making money; your eyes will soon be clear," over and over again.

Blessing considered leaving her husband quietly and taking their children with her. Her husband had remained cold to her from December 1998 when she moved to join him in Bonny Island, until August 1999. She cooked, he ate, and that was it.

Blessing had a friend in London who was willing to help her make a fresh start. So, she began to make plans little by little. Then, one Sunday afternoon, the family were all sitting together watching Pastor Chris Oyakhilome on TV, when he said. "You're a family of five sitting down and watching me now; you, the wife, you're wearing a purple dress and you have decided to divorce your husband. Please don't do it. It's not God's will for you."

Blessing (who was wearing a purple dress which she had worn to church) was sure the message was for her. She was so sure that her husband and children felt the same. So wanting confirmation, she prayed all week for the man of God to repeat the message if, indeed, it was meant for her.

The next Sunday afternoon, as the family sat together again, the pastor appeared on TV. His first words were: "God says to tell you, that family of five, you asked God to repeat the message today if it is you, so I am saying it again: God doesn't want you to divorce." That settled it for Blessing – she stayed. Mysteriously, Hamza changed, and started treating her nicely.

A CLOSE CALL

You have made known to me the paths of life... (Acts 2:28)

For a while after Blessing received the prophecy from Pastor Oyakhilome, the marriage was happier and her husband was kinder. But it became clear that Hamza had a girlfriend on the island, who he would see in the evenings or after dropping Blessing and their youngest son at church. People would tell her they had seen Hamza with another woman, but when she confronted him about it, he would deny everything.

Blessing's prayer was that Hamza would be posted overseas so the family could leave the island and possibly put an end to his other relationship.

As the new year arrived in 2002, Blessing flew to London to shop in the January sales. On the 25th, she flew back home, still haunted by a vivid dream she'd had - seeing herself wrapped in bloody towels as her husband lay on their bed just staring at her. Shortly before her return flight, she felt the

Lord say to her, "When you get home, do not drive your car. Anoint it and leave it for at least three days."

On her arrival back to Bonny Island, Hamza was not there to pick her up from the Jetty and was not at home either. Intent on attending church, she presented Barnabas with a large tube of Smarties, bought for him from duty-free at the airport. Then, she set off on her own. A decision she understood later.

As she approached a roundabout, she heard: "The Lord is my shepherd, I shall not want." As she thought, "What could this mean at this time?", behold a fatal head-on collision with a trailer; it could only have been God that she was not killed. The next thing she knew, her door was thrown open by a man she recognised – her son's lesson tutor – who had just left Blessing's house when he saw the accident.

He immediately started pulling her out of the car, but she couldn't move her right leg, which was visibly broken. He had to lift her out and carry her onto a bus that had emptied out all passengers to carry her and was ordered to go straight to the clinic.

Blessing could feel heat rising in her stomach and she was worried she might be bleeding internally. She kept pleading the blood of Jesus aloud, and those with her on the bus kept praying: "You are covered by the blood of Jesus; you shall not die but live to declare the goodness of the Lord." So, they got to the clinic to meet the unlikely; there was a full medical team ready to attend to Blessing. It could only have been God!

In the aftermath, the tutor raced back to the house in vain hopes of finding Hamza, the unbelievably absent husband. The church members had swiftly responded since they had been praying against death for Blessing when the news came.

They promptly went to the hospital, transforming the waiting room into a prayer service; it was like a revival had broken out as they prayed, shouted and sang. But Hamza was nowhere to be found. As night fell, his boss sent a driver to his girlfriend's house to tell him what had happened. He then went home to pick Barnabas in order for them to go to the clinic.

Blessing had an operation to put a plate in her leg and then after three weeks in the hospital, she was able to go home. After about 14 weeks, as she attempted to start stepping down, the nail implant popped to her hip, dislocating from the femur, leading the doctors to operate on Blessing a second time to take it out. So, in May of that same 2002, she underwent further surgery – to put a new plate in her shattered femur. The marathon procedure lasted from 9 a.m. until 6 p.m., and two of her church members stood praying at the theatre door.

Afterwards, the Anaesthetist said to her, "Keep serving your God; you would have died during the operation, but we saw your God."

Come July, it was time again to try to step down. But the pain was agonising and there were signs that Blessing's leg was infected. It was then that Hamza's project manager came in. He was a Christian who had visited her severally in hospital following the accident. He mentioned that Hamza's name had been on the organogram for the London office for over a year, and he was now planning to send him to take up the post in England. That way, he said, Blessing could get her leg treated in the UK (the company had already offered to fly her to Germany for an operation, but her husband had refused.)

When, a month later, Hamza's manager asked him if he thought the family would be ready to move to England in September, Hamza said, "Blessing would leave tomorrow given the chance."

The family needed to go to Lagos to get their visas and decided to visit Hamza's mother while they were there. His family had never tried to hide their dislike for her or the children, so each time Blessing went to see her, she would pray for God to help her say the right thing and to keep her from causing offence. However, it made little difference. As they arrived, Blessing set aside her crutches and knelt to greet her mother-in-law. "Mmmhmm," she said, barely acknowledging her presence.

Behind her was her husband – who was quickly embraced by his mother – and the children who, like her, were subjected to a cold greeting from their grandmother. Oh, what sadness!

For the entire visit, Hamza's mother spoke only to her son; there was no "I will miss you" or hugs for her grandchildren. As the family was leaving, Blessing again greeted and thanked her mother-in-law, but she received no goodbye in return. Not long afterwards, on the 15th of September 2002, the family of five moved to England with Blessing ready to put all bad experiences behind her.

The satanic realm began to manifest more and more after the accident whereby if she got angry with Hamza and quarrelled with him, she would suddenly have a strange feeling, so she began to move closer to pastors, some of whom have remained her best friends to date.

SETTLING IN ENGLAND

My flesh and my heart may fail... (Psalm 73:26)

Upon their arrival in London, the family spent a week in a hotel in Earls Court while they looked for a place to stay, and then moved into a house in Harrow, near Rayners Lane station. Hamza was then sent to South Korea to inspect some equipment which was going to be sent to Nigeria.

While he was away, the plate in Blessing's leg broke once more – she was unpacking boxes when she looked down to see the shape of her leg had completely changed. The doctors found that the plate was broken close to her veins, so if she moved at all, it could easily cut a vein and cause internal bleeding. They also saw that her kneecap had not been replaced properly, so back into surgery she went. A thorough makeover it was.

After a few days of recovery, Blessing was well enough to be discharged from the hospital. However, as she was still unable to walk, arrangements were made for her to live in a ground-floor room at home. Her husband and sons would give her tea and toast in the morning, and then Hamza left for work while the children went to school. Then, she would be by herself and unable to fetch food or drink until they got back.

That April, her second son, Paul, was also badly hurt in an accident – one that God had shown Blessing in a dream. In her dream, she saw her son fall and remain lying on the floor in a pool of blood. Terrified, she started fasting. Three days later, Paul was on a school trip to Box Hill in Surrey when he fell down the hill and broke both his hands.

Thankfully, after three weeks, his hands had healed and he could go back to school; for Blessing, Paul not falling headlong on the concrete could only have been God's mighty hand.

That Summer, in August, the family went on holiday to New York and that was where Blessing's leg truly healed. Her doctors had all told her that the more she walked, the quicker her recovery would be. So one day as they were shopping in New York, a city that never sleeps, behold a power outage (14th August 2003). Everyone else poured into taxis and buses, bringing the traffic to a total standstill. Blessing's family chose to walk the two dozen blocks back to their hotel. As they walked down the busy New York streets, she suddenly realised that the limp that had plagued her for so long had gone.

The family went on holiday at every opportunity: half term, Easter, Christmas... to any place they had not been. They went to Orlando, Madrid, Paris and Rome. It was all so exciting!

About a year after they arrived in England, the family went to a photography studio to have some family photos taken. Looking across to her husband, Blessing saw her husband's aloofness and she prayed in her heart and the Lord said to her, "The beginning of the end", talking about her marriage. She carried on with her wifely duties as if nothing had changed – making the meals, doing the housework, and taking care of the children most of all. In her heart, she remained quite hopeful that all would be well.

Hamza's time living with the family in England did not last very long because in March 2004, he was recalled to Bonny Island. Blessing decided she wanted to remain in the UK to raise her children and to put some distance between her and Hamza; she knew he was responsible for all the unusual satanic attacks against their eldest son Azariah, who was in his final year of school at the time. Usually, he excelled academically but began struggling at school and failing his Exams. As God would have it, as soon as Hamza returned to Nigeria, Azariah was back on track.

To make sure she could remain in the UK, Blessing enrolled in a local college and applied for a student visa. After doing short college courses in subjects like Health and Safety and Psychology, she enrolled in Bible College to study Pastoral Theology and then Christian Counselling.

After the accident, Blessing had not been able to travel to sell things back in Nigeria, so she had been watching her savings gradually become depleted. Although Hamza took care of the bills, she did not want to be totally dependent on him financially. So, aside from the two or three days per week dedicated to her studies, Blessing spent the remainder of her time working as a supply teacher to supplement the household income.

This meant that her children could eat better meals, not buying the cheapest version of every food while trying to keep the weekly shop to the barest minimum – she could afford the food that her boys most enjoyed. Praising God from whom all blessings flow.

Blessing was focused on making sure her children had everything they needed to do well, however, she was also careful to ensure they did not grow up spoiled. So even though the family was financially comfortable, she made sure the boys had responsibilities around the house.

It was only her second son, Paul, whom she worried might lose his way, as he fell into a bad group of friends and started ganging with them, missing lessons and misbehaving in lessons. His wonderful teachers would phone Blessing to say Paul had not come back to school for the register after break time, and she would go and look for him.

Paul and his friends would normally go to McDonald's which was on the high street, but as soon as they saw Blessing approaching, they would all start running. After warning his friends away, she begged his teachers to help him and to be patient with him, and Paul did settle down eventually. He finished his BTEC in Manufacturing Engineering and went on to university to do two degrees, proving God's power to keep His word.

All the years through and through, Blessing tried to protect her sons from all that went on in her marriage. More than anything, she did not want them to experience the shame she had experienced as a child, and she feared that, as boys, it would be even more difficult for them to grow up without a father figure.

Furthermore, God had told her that raising her children on her own would be a difficult task and that they would rebel against her, thereby making everything she had done to raise them in vain. She obeyed – she made herself blind and deaf to the actions of her husband, and she focused on God and her children. A decision for which she is eternally grateful to God.

A BATTLE OF THRONES

"My times are in thy hand..." (Psalm 31:5)

Blessings's mother Dorcas died in February 2004 after battling illness for close to two years. And from then on strange battles arose from Hamza and his family who had seen her as being protected by her mother hitherto... Such ignorance... forgetting the God that neither sleeps nor slumbers.

Once Hamza settled back in Nigeria, they became less and less of a married couple and more like occasional roommates. Hamza's boss offered him courses to do in London from time to time, so that he could visit his family at the same time. But he always turned them down, claiming they were courses he had done before. But Blessing suspected that the real reason was that he did not want to see her and their sons. His visits became less frequent, shorter and much colder.

When they were together, physical intimacy started to feel like something Hamza was doing out of duty, and then stopped altogether – if Blessing moved closer to him, he would almost recoil, and he would only go to bed once she was asleep. When asked what was wrong, he would shut her down, leaving her to cry herself to sleep most times.

Even phone calls became less and less frequent: if Blessing rang Hamza, he would pick up the call and after a few minutes, he would say, "Someone is paying for this call." He rarely thought to pick up the phone to call his wife himself.

Blessing knew better than to pick quarrels because she would always be the one who would have to apologise. If she did not, the husband would give her the silent treatment that could go on for weeks – shortly after their first son was born, their two mothers had a falling out and Hamza refused to speak to his mother-in-law Dorcas for three weeks even with them all living in the same house.

It was not just neglect that Hamza was guilty of in his marriage to Blessing. Ever since the birth of their first son, and especially once they were in the UK, she felt Hamza was waging spiritual attacks against her and even their sons. Whenever he returned to London, she noticed a change in her attitude towards her children and in her eldest son's behaviour towards her; she would find herself getting angry and overly critical of her children. Then, she felt the Holy Spirit whisper to her: "Check your heart; you are being pushed to treat your children badly."

On knowing that, she made a conscious effort to love her children more whenever her husband came around, thereby making it impossible for him to come between them and making it difficult to attack their minds. Especially after one of her sons confessed that he always felt so much hate towards her as soon as the father entered the house.

Once Hamza had been recalled back to Bonny Island, the negative influence he seemed to have on Azariah's character and academic performance faded away. Each time he returned, family life, though joyous, was also very challenging, and Blessing cried out to God for Azariah: "Lord, please touch him. I cannot be suffering at the hands of my husband and at the hands of my child as well, not when he is the one for whom I'm making this sacrifice."

The answer to her prayer came on Easter Sunday, 2005, when Azariah was 17. That morning, she was putting clothes into the washing machine and as she took his shirt, she heard God say, "Upon this rock I will build my church."

"You have a great sense of humour, Lord!" Blessing thought. "He doesn't listen to anything I say." And off went Blessing and the children to church.

At church, as she knelt down and prayed, she heard: "Today is the day I will change Azariah." There was a visiting preacher at church that day, and as he got on the pulpit, he said, "Because of one woman here, God has told me to start with what we would normally do at the end." He asked everyone to close their eyes and for the worship band to start playing music again. Then, the pastor asked if there was anyone in the room who wanted to give their life to Christ. He said he knew that God was calling one young man in particular.

"The mother who gave birth to you has wrestled enough," he said. Blessing prayed earnestly that she would be the woman who had prompted this altar call, that her son would be the one to surrender to Christ, and that the messages she had had that morning would be fulfilled.

Suddenly, many came out and some encountered God there and then. Azariah included Everyone kept praying and when the time came to open their eyes, Blessing saw that her son was having a spiritual experience, the likes of which she had never seen before. She wept with joy for the rest of the day.

One of the most dramatic attacks Blessing experienced happened on one of her husband's visits. On the day he was to return to Nigeria, she broke her fast to eat with her husband before he left for the airport, and as was her usual practice, she went with a lady to the church for the midweek service as soon as her husband left for the airport.

By the time Blessing got there, she felt like a razor was cutting her intestines and someone was hitting a hammer on her head. She sat at the back of the church and lay with her head on the chair in front of her, but that just made the pain worse.

"Lord, save me!" she prayed, over and over. When the pastor was coming to the end of his sermon, she rushed to the door of the vestry to ask him to pray for her. "My stomach, my head!" she was crying as the pastor approached. He produced some anointing oil and poured it into her mouth.

"God saved you by bringing you to church tonight," the pastor explained. "You just ate with someone and you have been poisoned. That person has also been calling you just to know what has happened. But, know that Jesus has set you free."

As Blessing drank the anointing oil, it was like petrol being poured onto a fire – the pain immediately became much worse. By the time the lady dropped her back home at 10 p.m., Blessing could not stand. She was crawling on the doorstep, unable to even put her key in the lock, when her sons spotted her from upstairs and rushed down to help.

Azariah, the eldest, told his mother to make herself sick by putting her fingers down her throat. Immediately, she threw up all she had eaten, with everything coming out just as she ate it, as if it had never been digested at all. After having thrown up, her body felt cool – the burning sensation vanished. And she heard Psalm 31 verse 15: "My times are in thy hand: deliver me from them that persecute me." Exhausted, she fell asleep while her sons took turns watching her. When she awoke at around 4 a.m., Azariah was beside her.

"Mum," he said, "Daddy has been calling during the night – we don't know why because he never calls when he is travelling until the morning he arrives. But he was asking where you were and why your phone was switched off." With that, the words of the pastor the previous evening were just playing in her head She checked her phone and, just as he had said, there were ten missed calls from her husband.

She did not want to panic her children so she kept everything to herself and when Hamza rang her again on arrival in Nigeria she behaved as if nothing had happened: "Thank God for another safe journey. How are you?" she said.

When she hung up, tears rolled down her face. "Why God? Why?" she wept.

CAST ASIDE

Take counsel together; and it shall come to nought... (Isaiah 8:-10)

Hamza's warmth toward his wife was selective, emerging only when he sought something from her. For instance, facing difficulties at work, he would quickly turn to her seeking advice and comfort, requesting her prayers. He was also warmer when it suited his interests to present a picture of family harmony.

This was the case when, in February 2008, Hamza's mother died, and he wanted her to be by his side for the ceremonies. Blessing stayed in Lagos with her husband for several days of mourning, returned to the UK, and was back again in Lagos for the 40 days after the Muslim ceremony of her mother-in-law's death.

During those weeks, Hamza and Blessing looked like a normal couple. But as soon as the ceremonies were over, life went back to the way it had been – with Blessing and her sons in London and her husband in Nigeria, keeping her at arm's length. She, as always, felt used.

Another season started with Hamza not wanting to book the Boat or flight for Blessing and the boys when they flew out to see him. That was getting from the mainland to Bonny Island. He would make them stay in Port Harcourt for a day or two, seemingly because he needed the extra time to dispose of any evidence that he had been spending time with the other woman.

Fortunately, on one such occasion when Blessing and her sons were at the jetty, Hamza's boss met them and quickly, he arranged for them to go to the Marriott hotel, something the family was entitled to, and which Hamza never wanted them to enjoy.

Keeping the family waiting on the mainland became a pattern. Although Hamza would pay to stay at expensive hotels with other women, he always left money with the driver that could pay for the cheapest possible hotel for Blessing and the boys. Eventually, she stopped telling him when they were coming, which further damaged the relationship.

By 2009, Hamza's project manager sent him back to the National Nigerian Petrol Company, partly because the project on Bonny Island was winding down and partly because of his gross insubordination. Times like this, when he was unhappy with his job, were the only times he turned to Blessing in order that she would pray for him. Thus, she lived a lonely life, even as a married woman living with her husband.

Hamza was sent to work in Abuja, and the move represented a mixture of sadness and joy. Hamza's half-brother, Mobo, was also in Abuja after having been deported from the US. Mobo was Blessing's favourite; she regarded him as a confidante. But this was short-lived after Blessing suggested Hamza hire his brother to help him find a flat, so that it would be Mobo who made money from the deal, rather than an estate agent. Hamza agreed, but as soon as money began to come into his hands, Mobo began to break Blessing's confidence.

Over time, she realized that her husband was discovering things which she had only shared with his brother, and that meant the tensions between her and her husband continued to worsen. This was one of Hamza's lifelong tactics: when she became close to someone, he would win them over with money so that they were more loyal to him than to his wife and where possible, he would destroy them.

This meant that Blessing had to distance herself more and more from Mobo and ended up feeling even more isolated. Sadly, Mobo died very suddenly in October 2011; at this time he was no longer her confidante, just her friend.

Blessing's grief over her marriage came to a head when, a year after her husband moved to Abuja, he was sent to Brass

LNG's office in Houston, Texas. The plan was for him to have a stopover in London so he could see her and the boys: he would arrive from Nigeria at 6 a.m., come home and then leave back to Heathrow for his 10 p.m. flight to Houston. Sadly, it was not to be.

Blessing spent hours getting everything ready for him – cleaned the house, brought out her best tablecloth, her best china on display and cooked his favourite meal. She stood ready, wearing her best dress. Slowly, the time went by... with no call and no husband in sight. By this time Blessing knew she knew she had made a fool of herself.

She changed her clothes and thought never to cause herself suffering again, although she still held onto hope, thinking that perhaps Hamza had gone somewhere with his colleague before coming home. Hours went by and eventually, Blessing gave up and returned the feast to the fridge.

The next morning, while in class at Bible College, she received a message from a US number she did not know. "Good morning," it said. "We are now in the US. I just got to the office and I have been given this phone, so save the number." Her eyes immediately filled with tears, prompting one of her classmates to ask her what was wrong. Not yet ready to open up, she pretended there was just something in her eye and excused herself to the bathroom. There, she gathered her thoughts and washed and powdered her face so she could go back to class as if nothing had happened. But inside, sorrow filled her heart.

She remembered their 10th anniversary when she had come to London on business and Hamza was coming back from Japan. He had promised to call her so they could spend the day together. But, just like this time, he did not call. Instead, he spent the night alone in the hotel and went to Lagos the next day.

That evening, Hamza called her and gave her his excuses, saying that James, the other man he was travelling with, did not have a visa to enter the UK. He claimed he did not want to leave James at the airport by himself. That did not make sense to her: James was going back to his own family in Houston, so surely he would have understood if he had left him for a few hours to see his wife and children. But she knew better than to argue because what Hamza wants he does, so she went along with the story.

Hamza's project in Texas came to an end after three months. At that point, Blessing hoped against hope that he would stop over to see them in London this time before returning to Nigeria. Once again, she cleaned, she cooked, she waited. And guess what? He never came and his phone was switched off. Blessing was quicker to realize this time that he was not going to visit and she just let it go.

It was at times like this that she rejoiced at knowing God and being in the Bible College which became a place of succor. Although she struggled to focus at times, she was grateful to have people to pray with… Pastors!

Blessing knew she no longer had a mother to cry to, she had never had a father to protect her and she had no siblings to advocate her cause. Even some of her friends had fallen away when they saw her marriage begin to crumble; some felt she was no longer good enough to spend time with, or they feared she would cause trouble in their own marriages. So it was the fellowship she had at Bible college, the guidance she received from pastors and, most of all, her relationship with Jesus Christ which kept her going.

MARRIED BUT SINGLE

God setteth the solitary in families... (Psalm 68:6)

M arriage, they say, is honey to your soul with the right person and with the wrong person it is like having a serpent under your sheets. It did start so wonderfully until a little taking for granted, little quarrels, little belittling comments, little snares... the list is endless.

Initially, for Blessing and Hamza, it was sweet; they were a model family. He became a husband, loving everything about Blessing. And Blessing loved him beyond human reason as the husband of her youth; they laughed together in that special way. They lived in a close-knit relationship with their children.

But gradually, that changed. Firstly it was with extramarital affairs and silent spiritual attacks that seemed to be coming from outside, when actually they were coming from inside the family.

Back in 2007, God had prepared Blessing for a life of spiritual battles that were to come. She felt God leading her to buy a house in Lagos, but she was not sure if she had the money for it and wondered why she would need another house when her husband had bought properties all over Lagos already. However, Blessing took the word seriously and shared it with her old Pastor friend when she saw him at the Redemption Camp in Lagos. "When God gives you a message like that," he told her "He normally knows how He will provide for it."

"If you are looking for a place in Lagos," he continued, "you should get somewhere here in the Redemption Camp. It is the safest place. A one-bedroom flat here costs about 1.5 million Naira." Blessing thought she might have about 1 million Naira saved but still, they went into the office, where they met the Pastor in charge of the project and sales of the flats.

"Sister, what kind of prayer have you been praying?" asked the Redemption Camp Pastor in the office. While Blessing was still wondering what he meant by this, he went on to say: "Well, there were no vacant properties. But a man who had put down a 500,000 Naira deposit just came in to return his key because he cannot pay the balance. He just left — you probably passed him in the car park!"

Blessing explained that she did not think she had that much money. "No problem," the Pastor said. "Just give us the 500,000 Naira now so we can pay that man back and you can settle the rest later."

Blessing was over the moon looking around the flat and fell in love with it. It was a one-bedroom, two-bathroom flat with spacious rooms. She danced and gave thanks to God, but the next thing for certain was that she needed to go to her bank as soon as possible. Then she had the biggest surprise of all: when she asked what her balance was, the teller told her she had 1.85 million Naira. Miracle-working God.

"Are you sure?" Blessing asked. "Where has that money come from? I don't want to be taking someone else's money!" The teller read out the names – sure enough, they were all people who owed her money from buying her goods. So that very day she was able to buy the flat outright. A few years later, it would become clear why God had instructed her to get a place of her own. A place that has become her place of refuge over the years.

Hamza's retirement was set for January 2012 so Blessing went to Nigeria to spend some time with him in the retirement home he had bought a few years beforehand. It was a huge five-bedroom duplex set in its own compound, with two other flats which were rented. When she arrived, Blessing called Hamza's immediate sister, who was indeed very good to her, to let her know she had that she was home. She then found that she was being thanked profusely over the phone.

"Thank you, Blessing! All those people who said he should not marry you, they made a mistake!" It transpired that he had given his sisters and her three uncles a huge sum of money from his retirement package without her knowledge. She did not know how much money he got for his Retirement. Blessing also knew he had been buying the loyalty of family members – his sisters and Blessing's uncles – but she kept her cool.

"Don't worry, Auntie!" she said to her sister-in-law over the phone. "We're old people now, it's in the past. You're his blood so you deserve it."

The sister then rang Hamza to suggest the family go to church to give thanks for his career and the blessings it had brought, and then have a party to celebrate. Suddenly, he started accusing her of having come from London to plan a party which he did not want. Blessing was bewildered – she hated parties!

But even when his sister confirmed that it had been all her idea, it was too late; Hamza had stormed off, refusing to eat the food she had made for him. Then she thought, "Oh, he must be holding me responsible for his retirement."

With no idea where her husband had gone or how long he would be away, Blessing decided to go to her own flat in the Redemption Camp. But while she was waiting for the driver, she fell asleep and had a dream: bandits broke into the compound, came into the house and they were pointing guns at her. Then the leader came in and pulled down his balaclava to get a good look at Blessing. "No, I know her. I can't kill this person, God forbid," he said, and walked out.

At that point, Blessing woke up and decided not to stay a moment longer in the house. She had already suspected that it was cursed against her because when she opened the door to her room, there were bats flying about, while all the other rooms were empty. She was grateful for the refuge of her flat and, when she did not hear from her husband over the next few days, she brought her flight forward and left Lagos to be back with her sons.

After this exchange, the pair communicated mainly by email, only speaking over the phone if one of the children needed something. Then, one day in June of 2013 she got an email from her husband, saying that as he was turning 60 that year, he would like to celebrate his birthday, and asked if she could start thinking how they could have a small party.

What an irony, Blessing thought, remembering their last big disagreement had been about Hamza not wanting a retirement party – now he was asking for a birthday celebration. He had never explained why he had behaved the way he did the last time she visited. So, in her reply, she did not hold back.

"I'm very happy you are turning 60," Blessing wrote. "But we haven't shared the same bed in almost four years. So how can I wear the same clothes as you and dance with you?" She reminded him of her last visit to Lagos and how he had left her with no explanation. "So I will organize a party, only if you tell me why you walked out on me and whether you agree that we are truly married without having sex."

Hamza ignored her email. All his sisters by the same mother took his side. About a year later, Blessing's uncle and Hamza's half-sister tried to intervene by mediation between the pair, but it was hopeless. When they tried to get to the root of the problem, Hamza accused Blessing of not giving him notice of her trip to Nigeria.

"How is that a problem?" Hamza's sister asked. "That should be a pleasant surprise. Does she need your permission to come to her house?" Blessing's uncle asked him about why there was no sex in the marriage for so long: "Wouldn't you dissolve the marriage if the roles were reversed?" Hamza agreed that he would. Still, nothing changed. The bitterness between them only increased.

Sooner rather than later, family interference began to damage their relationship. Colleagues would report him for all the weird behaviours... It was Blessing who had to apologise to them.

He was neither Christian nor Muslim but chose Islam whenever convenient. Particularly as it permits four wives. It is a beautiful thing being involved with three women and faking being with one only... Haha!

Being in the Occult became obvious as time went on. One question Blessing ponders is, "Why Hamza, why?"

LEGACIES OF A LIFETIME

Like arrows in the hand of a warrior, so are the children of one's youth. (Psalm 127: 3-5)

For several years, Hamza never visited the family in England again. It was then that Blessing started noticing strange happenings affecting her sons. Azariah, for example, was doing his clinical placement in the US however, after visiting his father in Nigeria along with his brothers, Azariah found himself having to fight to get his US visa renewed. The American Embassy denied him twice without giving a reason. That meant he was stuck in the UK and could not complete the training programme which he was due to finish that year.

Blessing had her fears that it was Hamza, so when she felt God leading her to take Azariah to his father, she obeyed. They arrived at the house to find it empty. After hours of trying to reach her husband with no response, Hamza finally phoned to let Blessing and the boys know that he would be there the next day. Nervous about leaving anything to chance,

Blessing insisted they waited. Even the driver was ready to stay the whole night just to make sure they were safe.

Then came Hamza shouting as he opened the gate. "Why did somebody lock the gate? How was I supposed to get in?" He was ranting and raving, but it did not make any sense – the gate locked automatically when it was closed and could be opened from outside with a key, which they both had a copy of. Blessing knelt down, begging him to calm down but he carried on shouting. Then, to her surprise, Azariah said calmly and strongly, "Dad! Stop!"

Immediately, Blessing felt that something had shifted, and that the obstacles blocking her son's path would soon crumble. She and her boys decided to sleep in a hotel rather than risk staying in the house. That evening she prayed, "Lord, any woman I know that is hoping for a child, please help them get pregnant this night because I have seen what the Bible says, that your children will answer your enemies at the gate." Later, would hear that one of the friends she was praying for that night did actually get pregnant.

After she had prayed, Blessing fell into a deep sleep and dreamt that Hamza was outside the house in another temper. As she went to see what the matter was, she noticed his slippers were by the door. In the dream, she picked up the slippers and saw that her eldest son's slippers were glued to the bottom of his. She ripped her son's slippers off her

68

husband's slippers and immediately woke up singing, "Victory, victory, hallelujah!"

Azariah returned to the UK two days later and applied again for a US visa. Blessing was praying that this time someone else would interview him or that the interview might take place at a different office so they might finally get a positive result. And so it was. Azariah was seen in Belfast, granted his clinical visa, went on to finish his studies and had his graduation. How great thou art... Blessing sang.

Little did she know, there was a bigger battle to come. Azariah was back in England by June 2018, hoping to get a residency and be back in the US within six months. He filled in application after application but heard nothing back. 2018 passed. Then 2019 too. And in 2020 in the midst of a world crisis, the Heavens opened for him.

So Blessing was again sure she knew who was really behind her son's troubles. Blessing tried talking to Hamza several times to see other possibilities for their son, Azariah but her pleas fell on deaf ears. It was clear he was behind it all buying time for himself as per occultic practices.

As time went on, Blessing started to worry that Azariah was the only one of her sons who did not have indefinite leave to remain in the UK and, if he kept pinning his hopes on getting a job in the USA, he might not have a future in either country. At first, Azariah was resistant, being quite hopeful he would get a Residency place in the US and would not need to remain in the UK nor take the PLAB (Professional and Linguistic Assessments Board) tests. Eventually, he put in the application for the Indefinite Leave. Blessing prayed that Azariah would find the tests effortless.

And so it was. Did the Lord answer? He sure did. By the time Azariah had secured indefinite leave to remain and passed his PLAB exams, the COVID-19 vaccination programme was being rolled out, so he got a job administering vaccines. In a few days of being in this role, the management found out he was a doctor and immediately sent him to head a new location they were just about to set up in a nearby town.

At last, Blessing found relief after three agonizing years of seeing her son's dreams and ambitions stifled. For three years, he had been unable to practice, stuck at home with his mother, bearing the brunt of his exasperation.

LOOKING FORWARD

In concluding this first journal, I would like to say to the young men and women: Please never marry someone who your parents do not approve of... it's like walking on a time bomb with the name "curse" written on it. Remember, "Honour thy father and thy mother: that thy days may be long upon the land..." Exodus 20:12

To the woman who's already a wife and mother: Raise your children like they're leaving home the very next day with Godly precepts they will never forget. Psalm 25:4..."Show me thy ways, oh Lord: teach me thy paths." Raise them to be independent of you and dependent on God.

To the husband and father who is absent, spending money, not engaging and chasing his own agenda: Remember... Seedtime and harvest time (Genesis 8:22)

Marriage remains a mystery: how God keeps it, why He keeps it even as I keep journaling His grace, His power and His presence through it all. Need I say that my sons remain the greatest consolation in it all, with their lives showing me God's grace on permanent duty.

So, I can boldly say... I am confident that God who doth deliver will yet deliver.

ABOUT THE AUTHOR

Enibokun Tayo holds a Master's degree in Special Needs Education
from the University of East London. She has a passion for single
mothers and abandoned children, and her narrative serves as an
inspiring testament to the enduring interplay between faith and
relationships. Enibokun lives in the South East of England. She is
married with three grown children.

Printed in Great Britain
by Amazon

46357252R00046